To the reader:

Welcome to the DK ELT Graded Readers! These readers are different. They explore aspects of the world around us: its history, geography, science … and a lot of other things. And they show the different ways in which people live now, and lived in the past.

These DK ELT Graded Readers give you material for reading for information, and reading for pleasure. You are using your English to do something real. The illustrations will help you understand the text, and also help bring the Reader to life. There is a Picture Dictionary to help you understand the special words for this topic. Listen to the cassette or CD as well, and you can really enter the world of the Olympic Games, the *Titanic*, or the Trojan War … and a lot more. Choose the topics that interest you, improve your English, and learn something … all at the same time.

Enjoy the series!

To the teacher:

This series provides varied reading practice at five levels of language difficulty, from elementary to FCE level:

BEGINNER
ELEMENTARY A
ELEMENTARY B
INTERMEDIATE
UPPER INTERMEDIATE

The language syllabus has been designed to suit the factual nature of the series, and includes a wider vocabulary range than is usual with ELT readers: language linked with the specific theme of each book is included and glossed. The language scheme, and ideas for exploiting the material (including the recorded material) both in and out of class are contained in the Teacher's Resource Book.

We hope you and your students enjoy using this series.

A DORLING KINDERSLEY BOOK

DK www.dk.com

Originally published as Eyewitness Reader
Truck Trouble in 1998 and adapted as an ELT Graded Reader
for Dorling Kindersley by

studio cactus C

13 SOUTHGATE STREET   WINCHESTER   HAMPSHIRE   SO23 9DZ

Published in Great Britain by
Dorling Kindersley Limited
9 Henrietta Street, London WC2E 8PS

2 4 6 8 10 9 7 5 3 1

Copyright © 2000
Dorling Kindersley Limited, London

A CIP catalogue record for this book is
available from the British Library.

ISBN 0-7513-3147-3

Colour reproduction by Colourscan, Singapore
Printed and bound in China by L. Rex Printing Co., Ltd
Text film output by Ocean Colour, UK

The publisher would like to thank the following for
their kind permission to reproduce their photographs:
Key: t=top, b=below, l=left, r=right, c=centre
Pictor International: (14-15)
Jacket: **Pictor International:** front (background)
Additional photography by Andy Crawford (26bl & 32 bolt),
Ray Moller (30-31) and Alex Wilson (13t).

The publisher would also like to thank Rick Roberton at Western Truck Limited.
Special thanks to John Scholey at W Scholey & Son for the use of his truck, time and premises.

ELT Graded Readers

BEGINNER

TRUCK DRIVER

Written by
Michael Potter
Series Editor Susan Holden

London • New York • Delhi • Sydney

John is a truck driver. Every day, he gets up very early. It is 5 o'clock in the morning. He has a quick shower and cleans his teeth. He doesn't have breakfast at home. He climbs into his big blue truck. Today is a special day. He is going on a long journey. He has to deliver some important packages. The packages are not in his truck. He is going to the depot to collect them.

John looks at the map. He chooses a fast route. He is in a hurry
and he can't get lost! The map is very important for John.
He buys a new map every year.

The cab is full of dials and instruments. He starts the motor
and checks his instruments. Everything is fine! Then he looks
into the mirror. There is no traffic on the road. It's very early.

He sets off on his journey.

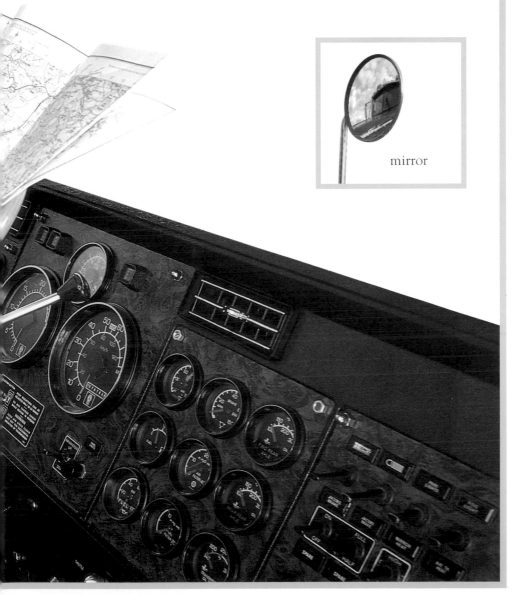

mirror

He stops at the service station. He wants to check the engine. It smells hot. He gets down from the cab and opens the front of the truck. He looks at the engine. It needs some oil. He puts some new oil in the engine. Then he fills up the fuel tank. He puts a lot of fuel in the tank: it is a big truck!

fuel tank

John loves his truck. It is very clean. He looks at the shiny engine.

"Don't give me any problems today!" he says.

"I can't be late!"

He leaves the service station and goes to pick up his load. He goes to a big depot. There are lots and lots of packages. They are not all for John! There are some other trucks at the depot. He opens the side of the truck. There is a lot of space. Now, he is ready to load the boxes. There are a lot of big boxes. A man in a fork-lift truck helps him. The truck lifts the boxes into the back of John's truck.

John sees some small boxes. He picks them up and puts them at the front of his truck. These are the important packages that he has to deliver. There is a label on top of the boxes. It says "URGENT! Special Delivery".

What is in the boxes? Why are they important? Who are they for?

It's 7 o'clock. It's a hot day. John is thirsty. He stops at a service station. He comes here every day. He drinks a glass of orange juice. He is hungry, too. So he eats some breakfast. What does he have for breakfast?

John is very hungry! He eats bacon and eggs. And bread and butter, and marmalade. And an apple! It's a good service station. John also buys chocolate. He likes dark chocolate.

Now it is 7.15 ... and John is waiting for his friend. Where is he? Why is he late?

Here he is! John's friend is called Paul. He drives a milk tanker. This is Paul's milk tanker. There is a lot of milk in it ... and the milk is very cold. Paul is taking the milk from the farm to the milk depot.

Paul and John are good friends. Paul isn't very hungry. He eats two bananas. What does he drink? Well ... milk, of course!

It's time to go. It's 7.30.

John says, "Bye, see you!" to Paul. He gets into his cab, and starts the engine. He waves to Paul ... and the truck goes back onto the motorway.

John drives into the city. The motorway is full of trucks and cars. It is 8 o'clock and people are going to work in the factories and offices. The traffic stops. Then, it moves forward. Then it stops again. John listens to the radio in the cab of his truck. He can be patient, but today is different. He is in a hurry.

The cars and trucks beep their horns and the traffic begins to move again. It is getting hot and there are black clouds in the sky. It's very hot in the truck.

John has to take the big boxes to a factory in the city. He wants to turn right. He puts on the traffic indicator and moves the big truck to the right of the road. There are some traffic lights. The lights are red. Now, they are green. He turns right and leaves the motorway. Most of the other cars and trucks stay on the motorway. This is a special road. It goes to the factory.

Soon he gets to the factory. The guard opens the factory gates and John drives in. He blows the loud horn on top of his lorry and waves to the workers. He drives to a warehouse. The workers are waiting for him.

They help him to unload the big boxes into the warehouse. John looks at his watch. It's 8.25!

"I'm in a hurry," John tells them "Please, be quick!"

But the workers are slow. They want to finish their cups of coffee and eat their sandwiches!

"Come on," says John "Hurry! I've got an urgent delivery on the truck."

It's 9 o'clock and John is on his way again. But there is trouble ahead!

What's the trouble? Why is John worried? Is it a problem with the truck? Or with the traffic? Or is it a different problem? Poor John!

John drives outside the factory gates. There is a van on the road. Its engine isn't working. John's truck is wide and the road is very narrow. That is the problem!

John can't pass the van. He puts on the brakes and stops. A queue of traffic builds up behind him. The drivers sound their horns. They are impatient – and some of them are angry.

He gets out of the cab. He is very angry!

"Look! Can't you get your van over to the side of the road?" he asks the driver.

The driver puts out his hands.

"Sorry," he says "I can't move it." John looks at his watch. He doesn't want to be late. What can he do?

John picks up his walkie-talkie and sends a message. He calls a garage. He knows that there is a tow truck there. He tells the man at the garage where he can find the van.

"Please hurry!" he says. "I have an urgent delivery to make and I'm late already!"

Poor John!

Soon he sees flashing lights. It's the big yellow tow truck from the garage! He helps the van driver to push the van to the tow truck. The truck lifts the van and tows it to the garage.

It is now 10 o'clock. John climbs into his truck and starts the engine. The cars in the queue behind him start their engines. The traffic moves again. John hurries on his way. But there is trouble ahead!

What is the new trouble? And it's only 10 o'clock!

flashing lights

Ahead the sky is very dark. John sees lightning in the sky. He hears the boom of thunder. Soon the rain pours down. He turns on the windscreen wipers. They move very fast. But John can't see the road ahead of him. He puts on the brakes. He puts on the truck's lights and grips the steering wheel. He can't drive fast. He has to drive slowly. There is a lot of water on the road. Cars pass his truck and water splashes onto the windscreen. John wants to stop but it is 11.10 and he has an urgent delivery to make. He drives on, but he is very tired.

"This isn't my day!" he groans.

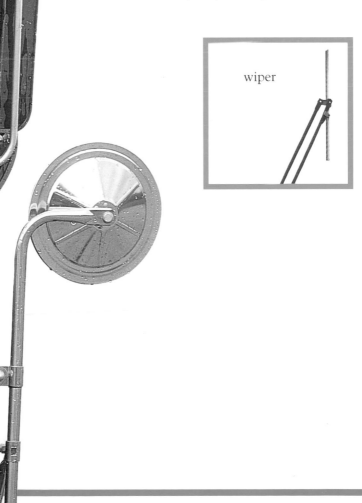

wiper

John drives on and on. He is tired and hungry! At last, the thunderstorm moves away and the rain stops. He drives into a service station and stops the truck in the car park. He turns off the lights and switches off the engine. He eats some sandwiches and has a drink of hot coffee. He feels fine, but he is still very tired. That is dangerous.

He can't drive when he is tired. So he decides to have a rest. He climbs onto the bunk-bed at the back of the cab. He takes off his watch. It's 12.15. Then, he pulls a blanket over him and rests his head on a comfortable pillow. Soon he falls asleep. Does he dream of traffic?

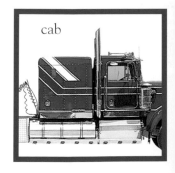

cab

He wakes up and looks at his watch. It's very late. It's 2.30 in the afternoon!

"Now I'm really in trouble!" he groans.

John drives off but there is trouble
ahead! He hears a loud bang and
his truck begins to slide over
the road.

"Oh no!" he cries "A flat tyre!
This isn't my lucky day!"

The lorry goes bump, bump,
bump. It is difficult to drive. John
slows down. Where can he stop?

wheel

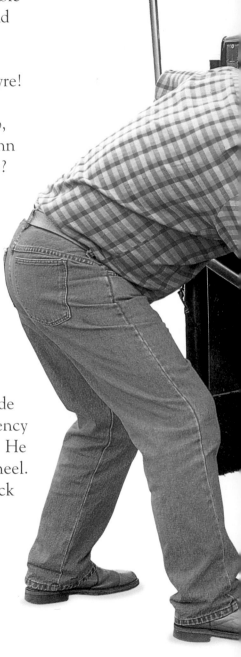

He stops the lorry at the roadside
and makes sure that the emergency
lights on the truck are flashing. He
grabs his tools and the spare wheel.
It is very heavy. He puts on thick
gloves and unscrews the bolts.

bolt

Then he takes off the wheel and puts on the spare wheel. He tightens the bolts and puts the tools away. Now he is tired again. And it's 3.15.

He drives on. "I don't want any more trouble!" he thinks.

He gets to a town and stops at some traffic lights. The lights are red. He looks at the map. He is nearly there! A car behind him beeps its horn. Now the lights are green. He can go!

traffic lights

BE-16-88

Soon he arrives outside a big building. It is 4 o'clock in the afternoon. He unloads the boxes with the "URGENT! Special Delivery" labels on them and takes them inside the building. What is the building? He can hear a lot of noise.

What is inside the boxes?

John goes up some stairs and along a corridor. There are lots of rooms on the corridor, on the left and on the right. These rooms are quiet. But there is a lot of noise at the end of the corridor. What is it? Where is John going? Why is he taking the special packages there?

John carries the boxes into a room. It is full of children. They are wearing dressing gowns and pyjamas. Some children are wearing bandages on their heads or around their arms. There is a little girl in a wheelchair, ... and a doctor, ... and a nurse.

John is just in time for the party at the new children's hospital. He helps them to open the boxes. The boxes are full of toys. There are dolls, teddy bears, toy trucks, and lots of other surprises. The children are all laughing.

"Thank you!" shout the children.

John smiles! This special delivery is very important and he is there on time!

"It's no trouble!" laughs John, "no trouble at all!"

Picture Dictionary

mirror

page 7

cab

page 24

fuel tank

page 9

wheel

page 26

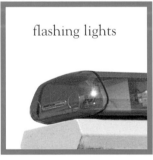

flashing lights

page 21

bolt

page 26

wiper

page 23

traffic lights

page 28